Mycopoetry

A Synthesis of Mycology and Poetry

poems by

Max Stephan

Finishing Line Press
Georgetown, Kentucky

Mycopoetry

A Synthesis of Mycology and Poetry

Copyright © 2021 by Max Stephan
ISBN 978-1-64662-469-0 First Edition
All rights reserved under International and Pan-American Copyright Conventions. No part of this book may be reproduced in any manner whatsoever without written permission from the publisher, except in the case of brief quotations embodied in critical articles and reviews.

ACKNOWLEDGMENTS

Acknowledgements to the editors of the following publications in which some poems, in part or whole, first appeared:

Appalachia: "Inky Cap Mushroom (Coprinus comatus)" and Part One of "The Naming of Names: Lichens" ("Metered Lichens") as "Names of Lichens"
Blueline: "Death Cap Mushroom (Amanita phalloids)"
The Broad River Review: "Truffles (Tuber magnatum)"
The Buffalo News: "Resilience"
The Christian Science Monitor: an earlier version of "Yellow Morel (Morchella esculenta)" as "A Mushroom's Retreat"
Fungi Magazine: "Bird's Nest (Crucibulum crucibuliforme)"
Kestrel: "Yellow Morel (Morchella esculenta)"
The North Dakota Quarterly: "Ode to Arik Roper"
The Wayfarer: "Shiitake (Lentinula edodes)" and "After the Wildfire"

Publisher: Leah Huete de Maines
Editor: Christen Kincaid
Cover Art: Arik Roper
Author Photo: Vincent Lopez
Cover Design: Elizabeth Maines McCleavy

Order online: www.finishinglinepress.com

Author inquiries and mail orders:
Finishing Line Press
PO Box 1626
Georgetown, Kentucky 40324
USA

Table of Contents

Discourse 1

Truffles (Tuber magnatum) 3

The Naming of Names: Lichens 4

Inky Cap Mushroom (Coprinus comatus) 7

Yellow Morel (Morchella esculenta) 8

At Green Heron Farm 10

Shiitake (Lentinula edodes) 11

Ode to Arik Roper 12

Flat #12 14

Lichens 15

The Naming of Names: Fungi 16

Bird's Nest (Crucibulum crucibuliforme) 18

Smut (Tiletia laevis) 19

Ode to Steve Axford 20

Wonder 22

Death Cap Mushroom (Amanita phalloides 24

After the Wildfire 25

Resilience 26

Mycology is the study of fungi, mushrooms, lichens, yeasts and molds: their identification, classification, edibility, cultivation, and biology.

Discourse

When you wake from slumber,
when your tender shape is eased
up from the underworld,
will you ache with wanderlust?
Or might there be a flash of doubt?

Will you opt to take a pew,
greet the divine, glorious rays
and praise the god
of whom you had dreamt
for months?

Or will the early morning mist—
wet, sensual—
caress you? Chill you?
Leave your soul
suddenly feeling complete?

Without warning,
might a flash of pride
overpower prudence?
Will an ache for independence
hastily take charge,
prompting a need
to leave the world of your creation,
the safety of your homeland,
your makers?

Or will the thought of rebellion
gently succumb
to the sheltered shadows
of century-old oaks?
The bounty that surrounds you?
The luxury of simplicity?
Seclusion?

Dear friend,
as evening's curtain is drawn,
will you bow with reverence, reuniting
with the soft, soft security of sleep,
and the magic
of months, and months, and months
of dreams?

Truffles (Tuber magnatum)

Pungent, ripe,
your chemistry brings rapture,
a need to unearth elation.

The aroma—
not fragrant, not perfumed,
but provocative,

worming its way through
grains of silt, of sand,
unconcerned about scandals on Fifth Avenue,
bills changing hands under moonlight.

What matters
is innocence,
the spell that makes
all nostrils flare,
pheromones run frantic
with raw, irrational passion.

But there is no hurry.

Deep in the forest,
undetected, concealed,
you relax—soaking up
pure bliss,
carefully sliding your tendrils
through darkness,
wrapping the roots of life
with delicate threads of silk

like a shroud.

The Naming of Names: Lichens

I. Metered Lichens

Sunken Bloodspot,
Rock Gnome, Gold Dot,
Trumpet, Wanderlust,

Black-eyed Boulders,
Southern Soldiers,
Grainy Shadow Crust;

Shag, Quilt, Dixie,
Wolf, Yolk, Pixie,
Monk's Hood, Witches Hair,

Bramble, Bull's Eye,
Bootstrap, Cowpie,
Dimple, Wooly Bear;

Specklebelly,
Whiskered Jelly,
Lipstick Powderhorn,

Sinewed, Pimpled,
Bumpy, Dimpled,
Bearded, Granite Thorn—

II. Free Verse Lichens

no doubt—the rhythm, scansion, pulse,
they're tight; no weak rhymes, sloppy sound.
But the down side is a pain:
When writing metered poetry about lichens,
the glossary of common names must be studied,
selecting few,
and scrapping all that do not meet the beat.

If seeking the perfect two-foot-trochee, say,
then *Blackened Toadskin* works.
But what about the misfits?
Deflated Tube? Potato Chip?
Foot count? Check.
But their accents? Not on track.

And how about the *Appalachian Camouflage*
or *Parasitic Firedot?*
They both define the trochee well,
but each walks with three feet, one step—
not two.

That's why, with lichens, free verse works the best.
Unlatch the meter-reading train of thought
when scripting life into the blue-gray tone of *Fuzzy Rim*—
or, go ahead and research tales
behind the naming of *Oregon's Cryptic Kidney*,
speculate on theories backing *Resurrection*;
add an adjective of five or six or seven syllables,
when comparing a colony of *Crazy Scale*
to an open jar of Smucker's
forgotten for a month.

Let the investigative mind run wild!
Be ingenious, crafty, sly;
ask, "Who picked goofy names like these?"—
then answer with an artful jab:
"Most likely an Alaskan trapper
who promised to keep his cold lips zipped
about where he found that *Frosted Finger*."

But in the end, with poetry,
the facts and figures behind the naming of names
are best if left alone—

for, deep in the Appalachian backwoods,
the next time you cross paths
with a red-and-milky-white *Jester*,
think about King Henry VIII's Will Sommers,
a deck of cards missing the Ace of Diamonds,
the blood spilled by the early, rugged settlers.

Inky Cap Mushroom (Coprinus comatus)

As if each hooded thumb had known
how brief, how brusque its breath of time would be
free from the sleepy, subterranean world
of worm and grub, root and slumberous seed—

what springs above the platform
of silky moss and lichen on loam
wastes no time—well prepped for swift retreat,
willing to leave nothing

but the remnants of autodigestion:
A weak, stained stalk soon subsiding;
its pale cap—stale, dissolving,
withering down to an oily, shapeless smudge.

The beauty each toadstool gains with fervor
will quickly slip and drain away;
its blotted shape curtailed, drawn back
to the patient, passive, tomb-like womb of life.

Yellow Morel (Morchella esculenta)

1. Spore

A subtle breath of wind
and fragments of hope
are scattered

lighter than particles of dust,
older than blood cells,
more patient than faith—

footprints shuffling genomes
to cracks in creek beds,
crevices between swollen roots
and weathered rock.

Most are led astray,
mislaid and forgotten—

but a trifle is found, coveted,
shrouded with shawls
of damp, decaying leaves

2. Mycelium

as covert work begins—

transcribing coded DNA into
intricate threads, into
growing orchestrated networks,
spreading its presence in the underground
among grit and grub, root and rot—

hoarding heritage
like backwoods loot,
forgotten cache
stashed away, protected—

learning from parables
of what is gained
through patience, precision—
the courage, the commitment
when called

3. Fruiting Body

to break free and rise,
to leap up from obscurity,
performing for those
wise enough to witness
the swift unraveling of magic,
the primal factory of life.

4. Decomposition

Yet it is not long
before true subsistence aches,
before its brief wake is cut—

metabolizing back down through
the silky moss, back down into
the forest's floor
to dream, and dream, and dream again

of what it means to briefly wallow
in such a feverish foreign sun—
to dream, and dream, and dream again
of light,
of wind,
of dew.

At Green Heron Farm
for Steve and Julie

No nitrogen.
No pesticide.
No John Deere tractors needed—
just one E-Z-Go golf cart works just fine.

No time cards keeping track
        of patience,
no supervisors overseeing
                      stillness.
All that's necessary

is a longing to wander,
carrying nothing but a wicker basket,
                pruning shears,
                knee pads,

            and an eye

for pins roused from sleep, creeping
out from deep inside the red oaks,
ready to show, to offer
what they have cherished
longer than voices and vertebrae.

True: When they wake,
when they wriggle up from their cozy burrows,
some hungry slugs might find them first—
take their bites of charm
without the slightest bit of reverence,
and then move on.

                      But no worries:

Go ahead—relax.
Have a seat in the meadow.
There's always plenty for friends to share
at Green Heron Farm.

Shiitake (Lentinula edodes)

The name alone makes your mouth water.
Go ahead—say it: *shee-TAH-ke*
The acoustics—foreign, curious, tempting…
the word's first syllable, *shee*—
soft, subtle, like a whisper;
but the second, a strong, bold *AHHH*
as in *Ahhh, NOW I get it*—
a class, a breed in a different league
far, far better than the button
sliced and diced on pizza pies.

When thinking of the Shiitake,
the taste glands fancy
Katsuobushi, Kombu, Iriko in Dashi…
the bold, brash savor of Miso Soup…
Buddah's Delight.
The imagination scribbles monks in saffron robes
foraging through the forest,
picking only those found mature, ready.

To some, this gem has forever been
the *Donko*—the Winter Mushroom;
to others, the *Huagu*—the Flower Mushroom;
yet no one yearns to know
the plainness, the utter simplicity,
of the name the world holds tight:
Scattered beneath the *shii* trees,
it is the *take*, the fruit, that calm hands pluck.

But, *ahhh, the Shiitake*—
to the palate, the chef,
its name translates as
triumph, as
faultless merit, as
desire.

Ode to Arik Roper

And like a dream, you see a child
sitting cross-legged with his mother in the Alaskan prairie,
watching her sketch mushrooms
canopied beneath tall grasses—
her eyes content, studying,
and studying,
and studying
the gills below the cap,
its texture, tones—trying best
to think like a beetle, a grub—trying best
to understand the rub
before resurrecting.

But there is no mother with you
in Brooklyn—somebody's house party
with some band jamming in one room,
drinks on consoles, toilet seats, kitchen tile,

and a heaping bowl of 'shrooms on the dining room table.

How many you had held
suddenly seems peripheral
as you lie still, voiceless, on the row house rooftop,
your memory hitting rewind
again, and again—seeing

the damp, dank network of new roots
you could not see beneath the Alaskan prairie—seeing

the fantastic—*fantastic*—underside
of an *Amanita muscaria*
looming—*looming*—above you
as if your eyes were the eyes of a glowworm—seeing

Psilosybe mexicane towering like masts, like steeples,
still feeling the burning sunset from hours and hours ago, whispering
No se sorprenda nadie porque quiero—seeing

as early morning light pulls you back,
like the gems you watched your mother sketch—
back down beneath the blades,
to settle,

                                                    lightless—

to hug the roots that call,
have been calling since childhood.

With nothing to confess,
no guilt, no weight,
this junction, this fork in comprehension
is where language has no use, where,
wrapped with the senses,

you are carried,
and carried,
and carried,

but never forgotten—

for what once had been carried,
and carried,
and carried in memory,
tucked away and hidden,

is now released.

Flat #12
for Robbie Gianadda

Just above the I-190,
a digital billboard in bold, black letters reads:
Flat #12 Mushrooms.

No slogan.
No catchy phrase.
Not even a picture.

Just words,

for the curious seek
what the culinary inner circle knows—
what Robbie grows
down on Mason Street,
just one block west of Niagara,
and a stone's throw east of the Black Rock Canal.

In plastic bags of clean wheat straw,
some mixed with millet, rye,
others decaffeinating coffee grounds from Spot—

what threads itself is
urban opportunity.

The life found
in lightlessness,
each breath drifting
in cool, cool air,
never needing to know
praise, prestige,
their rite of passage—be it

a Calphalon Classic in a kitchenette on Park Street,
the display case inside the Lexington Co-op,
a 4-star presentation at Patina 250.

Lichens

On concrete, cobblestone,
Jackson Pollock's grave—
furrowed bark,
fallow land,
old festered fence posts—

microcosms of speckles, flakes, dots
yellow, orange, green, red
bringing life to barren bedrock,
abandoned brownfields,
crumbling rustbelt silos—a conjuring

of esters from acids, cleaning
the contaminated, converting
the fragile, the forgotten into
calm, patient communes, into
self-contained cloisters.

The Naming of Names: Fungi

Some are nothing more than adjectives:
Slimy, Rosy, Woolly, Brownish;
others, telling verbs:
Glistening, Bleeding, Rotting—
no puzzle, no prize—all frank, simple.

But a handful carry weight—
heavy, *heavy* weight—
offering fools a fair warning,
if they care to listen:
Death Cap, Skullcap, Destroying Angel—
Amateurs: Don't dare to think twice
about tossing a few in your stir-fry
unless your Will and Testament is up to date

                     and waiting on the table.

In the kitchen there are
Lobster, Turkey-tail, Fried-chicken and Beefsteak
but never *Scrambled-egg Slime.*
Champignon for the French,
Kulturchampignon for the Germans,
Svamp for the Swedish,
but just plain old *Button* in America.

                     (Please, don't ask.)

Certain names throw sarcasm at opportunity:
Piggyback—a sound more playful
than "pinecone parasite";
a *Puffball* in the prairie, waiting for a hoof to hug;
or flashbacks of the Victorian Age
with *Girdled* and *Parasol.*
Train-wrecker? Check.
But no locomotives needed.

The odd meld abnormality with anatomy:
Blue-toothed, Cleft-foot, Black-nipple; Earth Tongue.
Others mingle imagination with mammalogy:
Goat's Foot, Pig's Ear, Dog's Vomit.

Eyelash Cup, Devil's Urn, or Slime Mold like Caviar,
Orange Peel, Blue-Haired, Wet Rot, Dry Rot:
These are the names the laymen know—
the backpackers and hikers, farmers and foragers.
Sounds that hum, tap, sing
of fancy, fun, of folklore—
like they've got something worthy to say
about forgotten Appalachian fables,

how the *Old Man of the Woods* doesn't mind a little company—
some comfort every now and then;
but after you've heard the stories experience has to tell,
its best to just leave him be.

For the naming of names isn't simply
the *naming of names*—
not the discovery of semblance in the obscure,
nor the labeling, the categorizing,
the ease found in an understood identity.

The naming of names is an admittance
of not knowing;
an abstract;
the revealing of weakness,
human insecurity,
the finite.

Bird's Nest (Crucibulum crucibuliforme)

Roosting in barkless trunks,
on broken, rotting branches—
not abandoned, not unwanted,
but left unguarded

without the warmth
of nestled feathers,
the calming rhythm
of beating hearts—

cupping mist,
collecting drops of rain,
allowing patience to break
the thin, fragile veil, remove

its mask, revealing
the modest rules of life,
the riches of humility—
an offering for those who choose to see.

Smut (Tiletia laevis)

Trash; garbage; dirt; filth—
or filthy; ill-reputed; rude;
unpleasant (but in a pleasing way);
to stain; to taint; debase; defile;
explicit; porn, or pornographic;
indecent; scandalous; sleazy; you slut;
rumours? what rumours?; with whom? and when?—
the whispered talk behind closed doors,
at bars, in cars, beneath the sheets;
defaming the famous,
                              exposing
what once was hushed, kept hidden:
Smut.

But this poem isn't about *that* kind of smut.
This poem is about Alberta's wheat fields,
Nebraska's corn.
This poem is about homes
bordered with barley, with oats.
This poem is about the titles
wanted and *unwanted, welcome* and *uninvited,*
and how blindly the masses follow.
This poem is about the naming of names,
the biases embedded in thoughts, words, labels.
But mostly, this poem is about fully understanding,
                        then accepting,
                                        or rejecting,
once all is seen through an unorthodox lens.

Ode to Steve Axford

In the Big Scrub Loop,
the Booyong Reserve,
what is found
you share with the world—

a showing, for some,
of what is not new
but ancient, primal,
thriving.

In Tibet, Yunan, Chiang Mai
you wander,

                                        gaze,

dropping to your knees
to witness
the timid, the unassuming,
in shaded chasms,
crumbling trunks,
the open—
dancing for no one,
nothing,
not even those who seek.

And when you find them,
eyes peek behind, beneath,
searching for the finite:
droplets caught during last night's deluge,
trails left by snails,
mist,

never knowing
who will decide to stir—
or when—

but fathoming
what each spore seeks,
what, sometimes, is best
if left a conundrum.

Wonder

There are facts that anyone
can pull up on their iPhone in seconds—
like how one single specimen in Oregon
covers 3.4 square miles
and is older than Christianity,
or how some frantic millionaire in Macau
traded $330,000
for a two pound truffle.

But not everything is factual.

Waking after 364 days of sleep? Fact.
Disbanding into an oily splotch of compost? Fact.
Though the mystery of what each mycelium dreams
month after month after month in the underworld—that
is best left free for the imagination.

I could try to sound philosophical, even perplexing,
crafting answers to unanswerable questions,
like *happiness, pure happiness,*
or just imagine the confusion,
the fear of a rookie
rising into some foreign world of chaos.

But answers are not what is sought—
not fact-based, provable evidence,

>   but pure,
>   unprovable
>   *wonder—*

like the *wonder* of resistance, or
submission;

the *wonder* of how far
a single gust of wind
will carry the last remaining spore—
clinging, clinging,
unwilling to let go—
then letting go;

the *wonder* of emptiness
when no more gifts are left to give,
no remaining reason to witness;
the *wonder* of what,
or who,
will offer comfort;

the *wonder* of language,
or lack of—
what caste of ancient, chemical communication
still whispers with root;

the fear of wariness,

envy of rain,

question of authority, empathy, age;

their take on deforestation;

the values of practicing magic;

the preaching of redemption.

And, off the record, *why Alice?*

Death Cap Mushroom (Amanita phalloides)[2]

Forget about the produce aisle—
you'll never find a *Death Cap*
imprisoned by bar codes,
pre-priced and packaged

in blue plastic coffins.
It's the envy of those domesticated—
mimicking its sleek, simple cloak,
but not its toxic content.

Each Death Cap holds no prejudice, plays no bluff
when fueling a fool's malfunctions:
At first a few obscured signs of falter—
a tad bit of slightness

irking muscles seldom used,
soon followed by a trickster's quick retreat.
Yet the final, fatal strike
lingers not too far behind:

The sudden heaving of blood, of bile,
the uncontrollable discharge of waste—
all as one's liver, one's kidneys falter,
and life expires.

---

[2]Primarily found in Europe, the Death Cap Mushroom (*Amanita phalloides*) is the deadliest of all toxic mushrooms in the world.

After the Wildfire

Like gypsies, nomads, drifters—
the foragers arrive under moonlight
pitching tents, parking trailers,
eager to weave their way
through virgin soot and cinder—
to trek between the black, barren pillars
in search of the elusive.

Laid off lumberjacks,
Asian immigrants,
traveling bands of Deadhead nomads—
some seeking challenge,
a handful drawn by delectable want,
others seeing nothing
but the dollar sign of Manhattan;

their lure, at times
the *Chanterelles*, the *Matsutake*
tucked away in shaded nooks
beneath thick, healthy greens—

but here
in this ghostly apocalypse,
in Montana's mad aftermath—
with all shades of thriving life removed,
with splendor wiped clean,

the *Black Morels* rouse
and rise
triumphant.

Resilience

For most, it is difficult
to find value in solitude,
associate with the term *discreet*.

Yet when magic is sewn
with pale, delicate threads
beneath autumn's felled leaves;

when patience is found tangled
in root-mangled loam—
defenseless, unguarded, brief—

that is when something of immeasurable worth
modestly offers respite,
consolation

on the fading separation
between steaming blacktop city streets,
and aging, untampered backwoods:

How to humbly subsist,
to selflessly co-exist,
to be.

Author of *Poems for the American Brother*, **Max Stephan**'s poetry and prose have appeared in a broad scope of journals, including the *North Dakota Quarterly*, *Appalachia*, the *Whitefish Review*, the *Christian Science Monitor*, *Kestrel*, the *Broad River Review*, the *Comstock Review*, the *Cold Mountain Review*, *Slipstream*, *Blueline*, and the *Cimarron Review*, among others. Recently Stephan won the 2020 Slipstream Press Chapbook Contest and was awarded Fellowship at the Martha's Vineyard Institute of Creative Writing. In addition, he was noted as a finalist in the Rash Award in Poetry Competitioin (2018, 2019), the Jessie Bryce Niles Chapbook Contest (2018, 2019), and the Homebound Poetry Prize (2019). Stephan teaches at Niagra University, specializing in Contemporary American Poetry. Learn more about Max Stephan at: www.maxstephan.net

www.ingramcontent.com/pod-product-compliance
Lightning Source LLC
LaVergne TN
LVHW041516070426
835507LV00012B/1621